Germany and Japan Attack

Sean Sheehan

Wayland

An imprint of Hodder Children's Books

THE WORLD WARS

© 2000 White-Thomson Publishing Ltd

Produced for Hodder Wayland by
White-Thomson Publishing Ltd
2/3 St. Andrew's Place
Lewes
BN7 1UP

Series concept: Alex Woolf
Editor: Joanna Bentley
Designer: Simon Borrough
Consultant: Research and Information Department, Imperial War Museum, London.

Published in Great Britain in 2000 by Hodder Wayland, an imprint of Hodder Children's Books

A catalogue record for this book is available from the British Library

ISBN 0 7502 2635 8

Printed in Italy by G.Canale & CSpA

Hodder Children's Books
A division of Hodder Headline Limited
338 Euston Road, London NW1 3BH

Picture acknowledgements
AKG London pages 5, 12, 16, 21, 23, 26, 30, 37, 40, 49, 50, 54, 57, 59; Hulton Getty 14, 18, 27; Imperial War Museum 35; Peter Newark's Military Pictures 2-3. 7, 11, 15, 19, 20, 22, 32, 33, 36, 38, 39, 42, 45, 46, 47, 53; Popperfoto 4, 6, 8-9, 10, 17, 24, 28, 29, 31, 34, 43, 48, 58; Staatsbibliothek Berlin 25; Topham Picturepoint 44, 54-5; Wayland Picture Library 41, 52. *Cover photographs*: Peter Newark's Military Pictures and Topham Picturepoint.

Contents

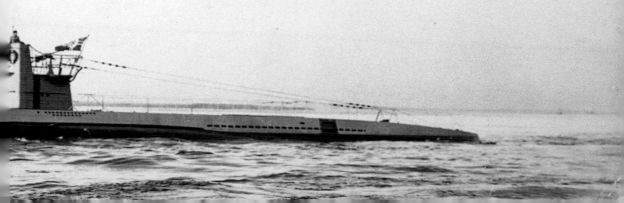

Invasion!

As the sun rose on 1 September 1939, at 4.45 a.m., German armies invaded Poland from the north, west and south. A small number of motorized and armoured divisions spearheaded the surprise attack. By 6 a.m. German Stukas, with specially-attached screaming sirens, were diving through the early morning mist to bomb Poland's capital city, Warsaw. These aircraft destroyed the Polish air force before it had time to get off the ground, and attacked railways and roads. The Poles resisted with courage, even charging on horseback against tanks, but because the German air force now controlled the skies above the battlefields they were thrown back, defenceless against the dive-bombers.

Polish troops on horseback were no match for the invading German army.

In August 1939, Erich Hoppe and other soldiers were driven close to Germany's border with Poland. They marched to a point where they spent the night, under orders not to light fires or make any noise.

'The next morning, just after dawn, there was a lot of noise and much movement as our panzer units moved forward. Then our lorries were brought up. We climbed in and set off . . . We were at war but there was no sound of conflict, except for a low rumble which could have been thunder but wasn't. It was gunfire, but very distant. There was a great deal of air activity, but otherwise nothing. That first morning of the war was a warm, bright, quiet and peaceful one.'

Source: James Lucas, *The Third Reich*

The conquering of Poland was achieved within weeks of that dawn attack. German tanks which had invaded northern Poland, with infantry accompanying them in trucks, sped south and completed a pincer movement, meeting up with invading forces from the south by 17 September. The chances of successful Polish resistance were further weakened when eastern Poland was invaded by the USSR, which claimed to be acting to defend members of Slav communities in Poland now that the country was without a government.

German motorized and armed units led the attack on Poland that brought the Nazis into Warsaw within one month.

The final assault on Warsaw began on 25 September. Within three days it was over. In addition to the thousands of soldiers on both sides who had died, the invasion also saw the large-scale slaughter of civilians. A special force, the *Einsatzgruppen*, which sought out and executed Poles likely to be possible future leaders of resistance, accompanied the invading German army.

In response to the invasion of Poland, Britain and France had declared war on Germany on 3 September. World War II in Europe had begun.

The causes of World War II

Consequences of World War I

World War I had begun as a result of the struggle for dominance in Europe between the traditional great powers - Britain and France - and new nation states such as Germany. The Treaty of Versailles, the peace settlement drawn up at the end of World War I, did not solve these problems. One French general described it as a mere '20-year cease-fire'. Britain and France benefited from the Treaty and, in the 1920s, had empires that would never be larger, but they were in economic decline. They had only postponed the need to accept the future power of Germany and other states such as the USSR.

History has not been kind to the Treaty of Versailles. It was signed in June 1919 but the ink was hardly dry before it became clear that political stability had not been achieved in Europe.

Germany, the losing side, was forced to accept blame for having started the war, and made to pay reparations to the victors. Strict limits were imposed on the size of its armed forces, with the aim of preventing it from threatening the world order in future. For many Germans, the Treaty of Versailles represented a great national humiliation. In the early 1930s, Adolf Hitler and the Nazi Party won popular support by promising to overturn the terms of the peace settlement.

President Woodrow Wilson represented the USA at the Treaty of Versailles but the US Congress did not ratify the Treaty nor approve American membership of the League of Nations.

The Treaty of Versailles

Part IV: Germany renounces . . . all her rights and titles over her overseas possessions.

Part V: The German army must not comprise more than seven divisions of infantry and three divisions of cavalry.

Part VIII: Germany accepts the responsibility . . . for causing all the loss and damage . . . as a consequence of the war . . . for which compensation is to be made by Germany.

The Treaty also created a League of Nations, an international organization that was designed to settle conflicts between nations by diplomacy. But it depended on the co-operation and goodwill of member states and lacked any real power. Not least among the League's difficulties was the fact that the USA refused to join. After World War I, the USA was determined not to be drawn into any future conflicts in Europe. This policy of withdrawal from international politics, known as isolationism, turned out to be temporary but, while it lasted, it led to instability in the balance of power. When war did break out again in Europe in 1939 the vast majority of Americans did not feel that their country should offer aid to Britain and France.

7

The Great Depression

The Great Depression was the international economic crisis that began in 1929 and was to last throughout the 1930s. The USA was the world's largest economy in the 1920s. Throughout most of 1929, the price of shares on the New York Stock Exchange kept increasing. Suddenly, in October, confidence in the value of US businesses began to falter. Prices tumbled, and continued to fall for the next three years. The effect on the US economy was disastrous. Banks, knowing that they did not have enough money in reserve to cover all the loans that they had made, began to demand repayment of their international loans. This was particularly bad news for Germany, which depended heavily on such loans.

As confidence plummeted on both sides of the Atlantic, ordinary people began withdrawing their savings from banks. The value of money dropped: people found that a dollar bought fewer and fewer goods. Banks continued to demand repayment of loans but this was not enough to save them and soon they began to close. Factories and other businesses closed down too because they could no longer sell their goods or borrow money from the banks for investment. Unemployment spiralled. Farmers found their crops and livestock cost more to raise and harvest than the price they could get for them at market, so animals were destroyed and crops left to rot in the fields. In Europe and Asia the economic crisis had serious political consequences, as people desperately searched for a solution to their problems.

Japan and the East

In Asia during the 1920s, Japan had emerged as the first industrial power. Between the two world wars industrial production levels rose five-fold and the size of its merchant fleet doubled. However, Japan faced a crucial problem: all the essential raw materials it needed in order to develop as an industrial economy, such as rubber, petrol and tin, had to be imported. Food for its growing population had to be imported, too, because

The launching of this mine-sweeper at Osaka in Japan in the 1930s was part of that country's determination to increase her naval power in the Pacific.

there was not enough agricultural land in Japan to make the country self-sufficient.

Unlike Britain and its empire, Japan's few overseas colonies could not supply such needs. Neighbouring China supplied much of its food imports and also had vast and untapped mineral resources, but the USA was keen to maintain its own economic interests in that part of the world. In the 1920s and 1930s, as China collapsed into civil war, Japan and the USA became competitors for influence and power there.

Such tensions might have been handled peacefully but the Great Depression changed the situation radically. Silk made up more than one-third of Japan's exports but, when the Depression struck, other countries could no longer afford to buy such luxury materials. The price of raw silk dropped by 80 per cent and many workers lost their jobs. Conservative business groups and the military found popular support for their view that Japan should find its own solution to the economic problem. If countries like Britain and France could benefit by having empires to which they could export their products, why, they argued, should not Japan also expand overseas? The process of imitating European powers by acquiring overseas possessions had started back in 1894, when Japanese forces occupied Korea. The temptation was to take this process a stage further and occupy part of China.

Japan's military leaders were also keen to challenge the terms of the Washington Treaty of 1922. This had set a ratio of 6:10 between the size of Japan's navy and the number of ships that Britain and the USA together could possess in the Pacific region.

Overseas demand for Japanese silk fell as a result of the Great Depression and silk-spinning factories like this one could not sell what they were producing.

One result of the Great Depression was that the USA put up trade barriers against Japanese goods and this increased unemployment and poverty in Japan. Arita Hachirō, a Japanese Foreign Minister, pointed out how unfair he felt this was:

'If any nation adopted a protectionist policy in contradiction to the free trade policy of the Anglo-American powers, it was ostracized and considered a heretic by advanced countries . . . Now, however, that such doctrines have all but disappeared with the Great Powers closing or threatening to close their doors to others, small countries have no other choice left but to strive as best they can to form their own economic blocs or to found powerful states, lest their very existence be jeopardized. There can be no just criticism condemning this choice of the small countries.'

Source: R.J. Overy, *The Origins of the Second World War*

The rise of Nazism

In Germany, one in three workers became unemployed during the Depression, and incomes were drastically reduced for many people. As in Japan, right-wing groups were able to benefit from the near-collapse of the economic system. Adolf Hitler and the Nazi Party blamed the Versailles Treaty for humiliating Germany and accused Jews of ruining the country's economy. Before the Depression, the Nazi Party did not count for much: in 1928, they gained only 2.6 per cent of the vote in Germany's general election. By 1932, this figure had climbed to 37 per cent.

Hitler, shown here reviewing Nazi party members in 1927, made skilful use of public appearances to boost his image.

The working class continued to vote for socialist and communist parties but the middle class and the peasantry, alarmed that these left-wing parties might gain power, began to vote for Hitler. Leaders of industry and business also campaigned to put the Nazis into power, knowing that they would crush the communists. In 1933, Hitler – quite legally – became the new Chancellor of Germany and, from now on, the Nazi Party was in control.

Hitler achieved what he had promised he would do. Political parties that did not agree with him were wiped out, trade unions were destroyed, and the Nazi Party became the leading power in Germany. The Great Depression came to an end and this helped Hitler enormously because employment rose and the economy stabilized. He made Germany strong again by drafting thousands of men into the army and rearming, secretly at first but then more and more openly. This broke the terms of the Versailles Treaty but Britain and France did nothing to stop him. Like the German middle classes, they too feared the threat of communism and felt that a Germany controlled by Hitler was preferable to one under the influence of the Soviet Union.

Germany in the 1930s

- The *Luftwaffe*, the German air force, had 36 planes in 1932 and over 8,000 by 1939.
- The German army, limited to 100,000 men by the terms of the Versailles Treaty, had nearly 1,000,000 men in 1939.
- The greatest number of votes the Nazi Party ever received in a free election was three out of every eight votes.
- In a research poll conducted in Germany after the war, over 40 per cent of Germans said they remembered the 1930s as 'good times'.

Mussolini adopted the title of Il Duce (Italian for 'leader') after winning political control in Italy. Like Hitler (the Führer) he was a dictator who did not tolerate opposition.

Fascism

Fascism is a term for a style of government that first emerged in Italy in the 1920s under the rule of Benito Mussolini, and later developed in Germany under the Nazis. Aspects of fascism that were common to both Hitler's Germany and Mussolini's Italy included rule by a dictator and the use of violence to crush opposition. Another common factor was an aggressive foreign policy that helped to glorify the nation state and promote the idea of a superior race. The two dictators liked the idea of empire-building and Hitler, who was a great admirer of the British Empire, aimed to bring the whole of Europe, including parts of the USSR, under German control. Mussolini had ambitions to restore the grandeur of the ancient Roman Empire.

The march to war

Japan goes to war

The Japanese controlled a railway line through Manchuria, a province in the north of China. They used this line to transport the goods they sold to China, and to carry imports of raw materials such as iron and coal. In 1931, the Japanese army claimed that the railway line had been attacked. In order to protect it, they invaded Manchuria. The government of Japan did not know what was happening until after the event and, when it did find out, did not feel strong enough to stand up to the military. In the following year, a government was set up in Manchuria under Japanese control.

As Japan's military authorities showed themselves to be stronger than the civilian government, the country became increasingly isolated in international politics. In 1932, the League of Nations judged that Manchuria should be returned to China but Japan ignored the judgement and, in the following year, left the League altogether. It called for a revision of the 1922 Washington Treaty, so that its naval strength in the Pacific could equal that of the USA and Britain, but the US government firmly refused to consider any change.

The Japanese army, seen here guarding their railway in Manchuria, drove the Chinese authorities out of Manchuria and ignored the protests of the League of Nations.

Upheaval in Europe

While Japan was challenging the political order in Asia and the Pacific region, similar upheavals were taking place in Europe. As the 1930s wore on, the world was heading towards war once more.

In 1935, the Italian leader, Mussolini, set about an invasion of the much weaker Abyssinia (modern Ethiopia) in east Africa. Like the earlier invasion of Manchuria by Japan, this was a clear test of the League of Nations' effectiveness in settling an international dispute. Once again, the League failed to act in a decisive manner.

Mussolini, driven by a vision of restoring the power of the ancient Roman Empire, delivered dynamic speeches to his black-shirted followers.

Mussolini's 'Dream of Empire' was outlined in a speech he made in Rome on 18 March, 1934:

'The historical objectives of Italy have two names: Asia and Africa . . . The aim we have in mind is the development and exploitation of the still countless resources of these two continents – and especially Africa – and of bringing these areas into the orbit of world civilization. Italy is in a position to accomplish this task. Her location in the Mediterranean, which is resuming its historic role of uniting the East to the West, confers this right and binds Italy to this obligation. We do not intend to claim either monopolies or privileges, but we do claim and we intend to make clear that those countries who arrived ahead of us [Britain], those who are satisfied and those who are conservative, should not try to block on every side the spiritual, political and economic expansion of Fascist Italy.'

Source: R.J. Overy, *The Origins of the Second World War*

Any lingering hopes that the League of Nations could deal with the challenges fascism presented to world peace were dashed early the following year, when Hitler marched his army into the Rhineland. This was a region of Germany that was supposed to remain demilitarized under the terms of the Treaty of Versailles. In the same year, 1936, Germany and Italy signed an agreement called the Rome–Berlin Axis. Hitler's confidence grew, and, in March 1938, the *Anschluss* took place, when Hitler's army occupied Austria and united it with Germany. Most Austrians were German-speaking and many thought it made sense to unite with the economically stronger Germany.

This photograph of Hitler driving triumphantly into Vienna in 1938 shows that many of the ethnic German citizens of Austria supported the invasion. The slogan in the background, Sieg Heil ('Hail Victory'), was often used during the Nazi regime.

Hermann Rauschning had many private conversations with Hitler and, in 1939, his book was published in Britain under the title *Hitler Speaks*. The following words of Hitler come from a conversation they had in 1934:

'We need space,' he almost shrieked, 'to make us independent of every possible political grouping and alliance . . . We must become a colonial power. We must have a sea power equal to that of Britain . . . We must rule Europe, or fall apart as a nation, fall back into the chaos of small states. Now do you understand why I cannot be limited, either in the east or in the west? . . . We must win the victory of German race-consciousness over the masses eternally fated to serve and obey. We alone can conquer the great continental space . . . We shall take this struggle upon us. It will open to us the door of permanent mastery of the world.'

Source: Hermann Rauschning, *Hitler Speaks*

The brink of war

There were also three million Germans living in Czechoslovakia, a country that had been created at the end of World War I. The region in which they lived was called the Sudetenland, and Hitler now demanded the right to rule this region. Britain and France had promised to defend Czechoslovakia's independence, although they were urging her to accept German demands. With Hitler threatening an invasion, Europe seemed to be on the brink of war.

In September 1938, the British Prime Minister, Neville Chamberlain, flew to Munich in Germany to attend a third meeting with Hitler. The French Premier, Edouard Daladier, and Mussolini were also present, but the Czechoslovak government was not represented in the main discussions over the future of part of its territory. Chamberlain returned to Britain with an agreement that he claimed would provide 'peace in our time' – an agreement that gave Hitler what he wanted, the Sudetenland. Winston Churchill, who would later replace Chamberlain as Prime Minister, wrote that, at Munich, Britain had had a choice 'between shame and war' and that 'we have chosen shame and we will get war'.

Neville Chamberlain claimed that his agreement signed with Hitler in September 1938 promised peace.

Chamberlain's belief that he had secured peace was soon proved wrong, as Hitler occupied the rest of Czechoslovakia in March 1939. Many historians say that the Munich agreement encouraged Hitler to think he could get whatever he wanted. It is also likely that, because the USSR was left out of the Munich talks, Stalin, the Soviet leader, felt it was necessary to make a deal with Hitler in order to protect his own territory. Stalin had earlier suggested making a defence treaty with Britain and France against Germany but this idea was not taken up. In August 1939, the Nazi-Soviet Pact was signed and a secret deal was made for dividing up Poland.

Poland invaded

After Munich, Hitler was confident that Britain would not keep to a defence treaty promising help for Poland if it were attacked. Thus, on 1 September 1939, the

Mavis Nicholson was eight years old when war broke out. She remembers the moment on 3 September 1939, at 11 a.m., when Chamberlain announced on the radio that Britain was at war with Germany:

'I heard the news down the back kitchen, on my grandmother's wireless - a big wooden set run on accumulators with the label: DANGER ACID - Do Not Touch. I was sitting up on her table watching my father shaving in a mirror on the door of a metal cabinet. He was in his vest, with his braces dangling over his trousers. As he heard Chamberlain's words, he nicked his face with the razor and said, "Bloody hell".

Source: Mavis Nicholson, *What Did You Do In The War, Mummy?*

Poland was invaded on the morning of Friday 1 September 1939. On the following Sunday morning, people across Britain listened to their radios and heard the Prime Minister announce that the nation was now at war with Germany.

German invasion of Poland began. But this time Hitler was wrong. Britain now knew that there was no peaceful way of stopping Hitler, and that unless war was declared Germany would take over and dominate the whole of Europe. Britain and France declared war on Germany just two days later.

Other countries in the British Empire and the Commonwealth soon followed Britain in declaring war on Germany. In this way, Canada, Australia and New Zealand became involved, as did India, which went on to produce the largest volunteer army in history, over 2.5 million men. The countries at war against Germany became known as the Allies and the countries opposing the Allies became known as the Axis powers.

Canada, Australia and other Commonwealth countries soon followed Britain in declaring war on Germany, giving truth to the sentiment of this British propaganda poster.

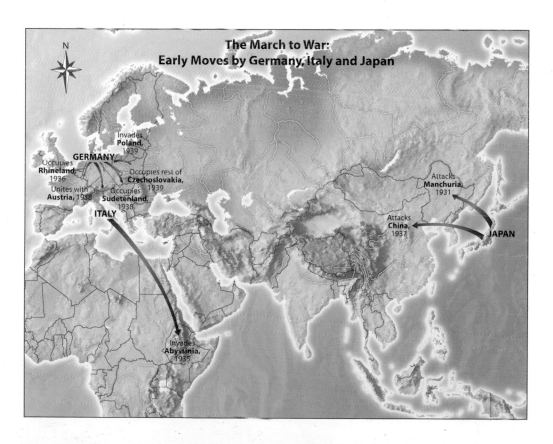

19

Germany attacks

Early victories

Following Germany's invasion and defeat of Poland, and Britain and France's declaration of war, nothing momentous seemed to happen. Britain sent troops and planes over to France but there was no attempt to engage with German forces. An air attack was ruled out because it was feared retaliatory bombing of Britain would cause severe damage to the country's morale. There was also a conviction that Germany's economy was about to bankrupt itself. An American journalist described the opening stages of World War II as the 'Phoney War'.

Günther Prien, the commander of the U-47 which sank the Royal Oak at Scapa Flow in October 1939, was awarded the Knight's Cross for his daring exploit. He died in March 1941 when the U-47 was hit by a depth charge, but it was more than two months before the hero's death was made public.

When action did occur, it took place on and below ocean waters. In October 1939, a German U-boat manoeuvred through a channel just 170 m wide and only 7 m deep, into the harbour of Scapa Flow in the Orkney Islands off Scotland. Here the British 'home' fleet lay at anchor, believing itself well-protected from attack. The U-boat torpedoed and sank the veteran battleship *Royal Oak*. It was a tremendous coup for the U-boat crew and an equally tremendous blow to British naval pride. Before the year was out, however, the Royal Navy located the German 'pocket' battleship *Graf Spee* in the South Atlantic. It was damaged in a battle with three cruisers and sought refuge in a South American port. Trapped there by British ships, it was blown up by its own crew and the captain shot himself.

Action on land got under way in 1940. Germany imported supplies of iron ore from Sweden via the Norwegian port of Narvik. To block this supply route, Britain began laying mines in the seas around Norway. But Hitler had already begun an invasion

of Denmark and Norway in April 1940. Denmark was defenceless and very quickly fell to the German army. Norway was conquered in eight weeks, with the *Luftwaffe*, Germany's air force, playing a decisive role. The British and French had sent troops to help defend Norway but the Allied response to the German invasion was muddled and ineffective. They were forced to withdraw, losing an aircraft carrier and two destroyers in the evacuation, although the already weak German navy suffered even heavier losses.

Britain's failure to protect Norway caused the downfall of Chamberlain and his replacement as Prime Minister by Winston Churchill. No sooner was Churchill in power than events across the English Channel demanded his urgent attention.

German troops march into Denmark in April 1940 Resistance was quickly overcome but the Danish king refused to go into exile and a government was formed that negotiated the best possible terms with the Germans.

France invaded

In May 1940, while fighting was still raging in Norway, Hitler's plan for the conquest of France was activated. The German army attacked France in two main movements: in the north through the Netherlands and Belgium, and further south through the forested Ardennes region. The British and French had expected a German attack through Belgium and had concentrated their troops in this area, as the Ardennes was thought to be impassable and was not so well defended. Emerging from the forest, German tanks, armoured vehicles and infantry crossed the river Meuse and were soon forcing their way towards the coast. The French were taken by surprise, having assumed that the invaders would head directly for Paris, the capital. British and French troops in the north of France were cut off from their supply lines by the blistering pace of the German advance to their south.

With the help of horses, a German howitzer gun makes its way across France in the well-planned Nazi invasion of France.

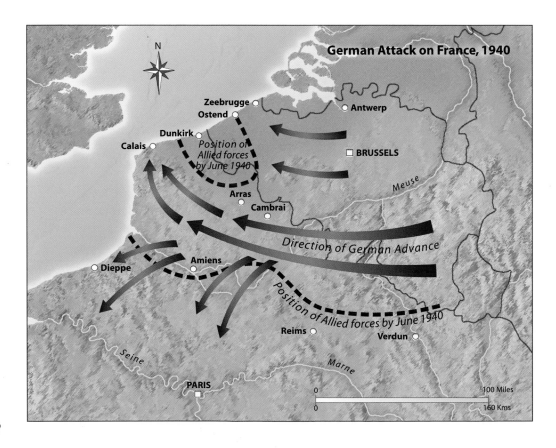

Dunkirk

Germany and her enemies had roughly equal numbers of troops and equipment but the Germans made better use of their air force and planned and co-ordinated their attack in a way that was far superior to the efforts of the Allies. The British were pushed back towards the coast. An officer, on being given a new map sheet of his area, described his realization of what was happening: 'Suddenly, glancing down at it, I noticed that a great proportion of the new sheet was occupied by the sea. Another look showed me a strip of coast. And the principal name on the strip was Dunkirk.'

Little more than a week after the Germans had started their advance across France, the British were forced to consider evacuating their troops. If they continued with the battle for France, they risked losing vast numbers of troops and Britain itself might have to surrender. They chose instead to occupy an area along the coast, and plans were laid for the British navy to evacuate the troops so that they could fight again. The decision was a controversial one, partly because they did not at first tell their French allies that they had decided to evacuate. The French army was left with the task of trying to withstand the German assault on their capital.

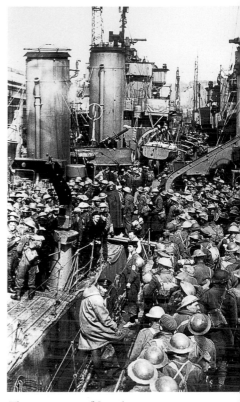

The evacuation of British troops from Dunkirk saw men crammed into ships and any available sailing vessels to get them back to Britain.

HMS *Skipjack* took troops off the beach at Dunkirk on 1 June and a crew member described what happened:

'Things were getting desperate ashore, the troops coming aboard were getting more exhausted besides being ravenously hungry. Loaves of bread were torn out of my hands . . . Survivors now were getting aboard in their birthday suits. We were constantly cruising about picking up individual Channel swimmers while our two 4-7 inch [10-18cm] guns were still hammering away at the Stukas . . . I heard our steward, who was an ammunition carrier, shout, "Ammunition gone!". It was still early morning when the German planes hit us fore and aft, and she started to turn over slowly . . . I remember looking along the messdeck from our starboard side and seeing all the troops sitting about asleep, perhaps dead. We lost 300.'

Source: A.J. Barker, *Dunkirk, The Great Escape*

Winston Churchill's 'V' (for Victory) sign to the British public became a symbol of his determined resistance to Hitler.

As the evacuation from Dunkirk got under way, the British government discussed the possibility of making a deal with Hitler. But they still hoped that Britain might be able to hold out alone, with financial support from the USA. However, at this stage, help from the USA could not be taken for granted. The US government did not want to see Europe dominated by Hitler but many Americans still favoured isolationism. With presidential elections fewer than six months away, President Roosevelt was limited in the amount of support he could offer.

Winston Churchill

Winston Churchill, the son of an English lord and an American mother, was a political maverick - he often held different views from those of the majority in his party and had been a member of both the Liberal and Conservative parties. In the 1930s, few could have guessed that he would become Britain's war leader. Distrusted by fellow Conservatives, he vigorously opposed the policy of appeasement, fearing that it would only encourage Hitler in his plans to expand Germany's 'living space'. He attacked his party in government for failing to rearm the country. Events proved him right and this increased his popularity with ordinary people who warmed to his powerful speeches. In May 1940, shortly after becoming Prime Minister, he told the country: 'I have nothing to offer but blood, toil, tears and sweat.' Once again, events would prove him right.

The evacuation from Dunkirk surprised everyone by its remarkable success. Over 700 ships, two-thirds of them civilian, crossed the Channel from Britain and, in one week, around 340,000 men (including 139,000 French) were rescued. Although there were some examples of cowardice and outbreaks of looting, the self-discipline and heroism of many saved thousands of lives.

The last evacuations took place on 4 June and the battle for France entered its final stage. Within a week, German success led to a French capitulation. Mussolini, keen to enjoy the spoils of war now that Hitler seemed unbeatable, declared war on Britain and France before the end of June 1940.

Nazi Europe

The fall of France meant that Europe, from Poland to the Atlantic, was under Nazi domination. Racist policies and the idea that white 'pure-bred' Germans were a master race led to an astonishing level of brutality, especially in eastern Europe. In Poland six million people, almost 18 per cent of its population, died.

The victory parade of German soldiers through Paris in June 1940. France was now part of a Nazi-occupied continent.

The conquered peoples of eastern Europe, especially Slavs, were considered to be 'sub-human' and treated as slaves, deprived of rights and education. 'For them the word "liberty" must mean the right to wash on holidays,' said Hitler. A special force known as the *Schutzstaffeln* (SS) had developed into a private army dedicated to the application of Nazi ideas. Across Europe, a deliberate attempt to exterminate the entire Jewish race was implemented at the end of 1941 and early 1942, with the creation of death camps where people were killed in gas chambers and their bodies burnt in the camps' crematoria.

The path to genocide

An important step on the path to genocide was taken in 1940, with the creation of special areas in the poorer districts of Polish cities, to which Jews were to be transported and confined. These areas were called ghettos, a name given to the traditional Jewish areas of cities where Jews had first been confined as long ago as the sixteenth century. Conditions in the ghettos were kept deliberately inhuman, with gross overcrowding and inadequate food. Anyone trying to escape was shot. The largest ghetto, in Warsaw, originally contained over half a million Jews squeezed into an area of 3.5 square kilometres. By the time the Germans destroyed the ghetto 18 months later, only 45,000 were still alive.

Jews across Nazi Europe were forced to wear the Star of David, the symbol of the Jewish religion.

Conquered countries were not all treated in the same way. Denmark, for instance, was allowed to keep its own army and government until 1943, when the Germans took over the running of the country. Following the French surrender, the northern half of France was occupied by German troops. A French government, based at Vichy, was allowed to run southern France, but strictly under German terms. Most countries in the French Empire followed the lead of the Vichy government in accepting German authority. As well as areas of North Africa, these also included colonies in south-east Asia.

With France under German control there was a danger that the French fleet, anchored off North Africa, might be used against Britain in the Mediterranean. This would threaten Britain's control of Egypt, the oil supplies in the Middle East and the route through the Suez Canal to India, and the colonies in the Pacific region. The British demanded that the French fleet surrender. When it refused, the British navy destroyed three French warships. In less than ten minutes nearly 1,300 French sailors lost their lives.

A familiar scene across Europe in the middle of 1940, as a German officer delivers orders to a defeated army. The man on the right is General Jakobson of the Danish army.

After the defeat of France, people thought it would not be long before German troops would land on the beaches of southern Britain. Here, British soldiers on the coast learn how to make and use petrol bombs.

Germany attacks Britain

Hitler did not think Britain could fight alone for very long. He gave the order to plan an invasion of the country from northern France. However, rather than risk everything on a major seaborne invasion, the *Luftwaffe* was again brought into action. The aim was to destroy Britain's air force, so that the country would be virtually defenceless when the invasion occurred. The British feared that they could not defeat the German army if it ever landed and so everything depended on the outcome of the battle in the air.

Fear of invasion

Once France had fallen, it seemed only a matter of time before the south coast of England was invaded by German troops. Schools on the coast were closed down and parents advised to send their children away. There were countless reports of parachutes being seen to land, although these sightings all proved to be imaginary. One woman remembered talk of how the enemy would 'come and deceive us by being dressed as nurses, monks or nuns with collapsible bicycles concealed beneath their habits.' Government posters appeared, with the slogan CARELESS TALK COSTS LIVES and showing Hitler and Goering listening to two gossiping housewives in a bus. Advertisements showed pictures of the kind of people who could lower the morale of the public: Miss Leaky Mouth, Miss Teacup Whisper, Mr Knowall and Mr Glumpot.

The Battle of Britain

The air war, called the Battle of Britain, reached its climax in August 1940. British Hurricanes and Spitfires met waves of attacking Messerschmitts and other aircraft. The use of radar gave the British warning of incoming attacks but the outcome of the battle was a very close call. Some 300 Hurricanes and Spitfires were lost in August. Then, in September, the *Luftwaffe* decided to switch from attacking airfields to attacking London itself. In the first such raid 348 German bombers with more than 600 fighters protecting them appeared out of the clouds. A historian of the battle described the sight, as experienced by the British pilots who had to meet them, as 'a tidal wave of aircraft, towering above them rank upon rank, more than a mile-and-a-half high and covering 800 square miles, blotting out the sky like some vast, irresistible migration.'

The battle in the skies over southern England did not produce the knock-out blow that Hitler had anticipated. Before the end of September 1940, Hitler had postponed, indefinitely as it turned out, the planned invasion. Nearly 20 per cent of the 507 pilots who died fighting the *Luftwaffe* were not British – Poles, Canadians, Irish, Australians, New Zealanders and French all played a part. Churchill, whose stirring speeches contributed a great deal to his country's stiffening resistance, summed up the contribution of all of them in a famous remark: 'Never in the field of human conflict was so much owed by so many to so few.'

Fighter pilots race to their machines to take off at the start of the four-month Battle of Britain in 1940. After the defeat of Dunkirk, this was Britain's 'Finest Hour'.

German bombing raids destroyed large areas of Britain's major cities.

The Blitz

In September 1940, Germany began a sustained campaign of night bombing that lasted until mid-May of the following year. It became known in Britain as 'the Blitz', short for *Blitzkrieg*, German for lightning war. The *Luftwaffe's* aim, broadly, was to destroy commercial and military targets but many bombs missed their targets and civilians bore the brunt of the attacks. Many cities were attacked, especially London, which, apart from a single night's break, was bombed for 68 nights in succession. An attack on Belfast, which had taken no precautions against air raids, claimed the lives of at least 900 people and caused a fire that could be seen 65 km away. The authorities at first tried to prevent people in London from taking refuge at night in the underground stations, because they feared that Londoners might refuse to leave the

Ed Murrow was an American journalist working for CBS in London during the Blitz. His compassionate broadcasts helped create a shift in American public opinion about the need to oppose Hitler:

'One bombed house looks pretty much like another bombed house. So it's about the people I'd like to talk, the little people who live in those little houses, who have no uniforms and get no decoration for bravery. Those men whose only uniform was a tin hat were digging unexploded bombs out of the ground this afternoon. There were two women who gossiped across a narrow strip of tired brown grass that separated their two houses. They didn't have to open their kitchen windows in order to converse. The glass had been blown out . . . Those people were calm and courageous. About an hour after the All Clear had sounded they were sitting in their deckchairs on their lawns, reading the Sunday papers.'

Source: Ronald Blythe, *Private Words*

safety of the shelters and go to work the next day. However, they were soon forced to give in and thousands crowded on to the underground platforms every night.

People who lived through the Blitz have vivid memories of the experience. One woman described the sound just before a bomb exploded as being 'as if someone was scratching the sky with a broken nail', and there are many accounts of the strange sense of excitement and common purpose that the bombing brought to people's lives.

More than 40,000 civilians lost their lives in the Blitz but the morale of the public was not broken. Nor was the impact on Britain's industries as severe as Germany had hoped. The war in the Atlantic would later come a lot closer to crippling Britain but Hitler could not predict this.

War in the Atlantic

With Europe under Nazi control, Britain depended for its survival on supplies of essential materials being transported in merchant ships across the Atlantic from North America. To try to cut off this vital lifeline, the Germans used U-boats to hunt down and sink these ships. Their efforts were so successful that Britain's survival hung in the balance.

Bombing raids on Britain took place at night and the following morning the damage was surveyed. 'Every morning one is pleased to see one's friends appearing again', wrote a Londoner in his diary.

Roosevelt was re-elected as President of the USA in November 1940. Strengthened by his victory, he was now able to offer more help to Britain. The US helped to protect merchant shipping in the western Atlantic by warning ships when U-boats were around. Out in the mid-Atlantic, however, the ships were still easy prey for U-boats hunting in 'packs'. Only when they began travelling in convoy with warships for protection were more ships able to get through.

The level of US assistance was greatly increased when Roosevelt's Lend-Lease Act came into operation in March 1941. This allowed the USA to lend or lease material to Britain in return for a promise of payment after the war. It marked a decisive shift away from the previous policy of isolationism but Roosevelt expressed it in a more homely way, by saying that if a neighbour's house was on fire it made sense to lend a hosepipe.

U-boat life

Life in a U-boat was spartan. Space was extremely cramped, there were no bathing facilities, and when a U-boat was diving even the one toilet could not be used. A lack of fresh water meant that the crew could rarely change into fresh clothes and most grew beards rather than shave. There was no rigid uniform code. Most of a U-boat's voyage was spent on the sea's surface and crew keeping watch on deck often had to be secured to the hull by a harness because of the danger of being washed away by waves.

In August 1940, Hitler ordered unrestricted submarine attacks on British shipping in the Atlantic. At one stage ships were being lost at a faster rate than they could be replaced, and 77,000 British sailors died before the German submarine ceased to be a threat.

The war heats up

Although the *Luftwaffe* had failed to defeat Britain in the skies, Hitler was not too concerned about having to postpone his planned invasion. His main ambition was to advance eastwards into the USSR. Once the vast resources of the Soviet Union had been conquered, it seemed clear that Britain would be forced to strike a deal. Before the invasion of the USSR took place, however, Italy's declaration of war broadened and complicated the course of World War II.

War in North Africa

Mussolini's decision to join Germany in war strengthened Hitler's position at first. In September 1940, a Three-Power Pact was signed between Germany, Italy and Japan, with the intention of putting pressure on Britain and acting as a warning to the USA to keep out of the war. In the same month, Italian forces in North Africa crossed the border from Libya into Egypt. Although Egypt had a limited form of independence, it was still very much under the control of Britain, which kept forces there. Britain's determination to resist the Italian advance opened up a new theatre of war: desert warfare.

German and Italian soldiers putting their artillery into position during the siege of the port of Tobruk on the Libyan coast of North Africa.

Soldiers in the desert of North Africa try their hand at mixing pastry. Keeping troops supplied with food and fresh water was a major problem in the desert.

The German general, Erwin Rommel, described the desert as 'a tactician's paradise and a quartermaster's hell'. By paradise he was referring to the conditions for planning the movement of troops and weaponry. Nearly all of the desert war took place in a coastal strip of sand some 65 km wide, which was mostly uninhabited except for soldiers and their armoured units. Tactical battles became like giant games of chess. For a quartermaster (the person in charge of planning supplies), however, war in the desert was 'hell'. He faced the challenge of finding supplies of fresh water and bringing in provisions of food, fuel and equipment. This is why Tobruk, El Agheila and Tripoli in Libya became so important to the warring sides: they were ports and they had supplies of water.

In December 1940, the Italian advance had been halted and a counter-offensive was launched. By February 1941, a dramatic success in North Africa was achieved by Allied forces – British and Indian troops at first, with Australians and New Zealanders becoming involved later. Moving westwards to attack the Italians, they took 130,000 prisoners. This proved, however, to be only one advance in a long campaign that saw opposing armies of tanks and soldiers move forwards and backwards across 1,600 km of desert sand.

The situation could have been avoided if the early success in February had been carried through and the Italians completely expelled from North Africa. But the Allied advance was suddenly halted. Churchill decided that extra troops were needed in Greece and, as a consequence, the unfinished business in Libya was brought to a premature end.

Military mistakes were made by all the warring parties in World War II but the decision to send 60,000 troops from North Africa to Greece turned out to be one of the costliest. Hitler sent German forces under General Rommel to North Africa at around the same time to try to support the Italians, and with fresh troops, superior tactics and better use of weapons, Rommel found it easy to roll back the now-weakened British forces.

A long-term consequence of the failure to expel the Italians was that British forces had to remain committed to fighting in North Africa. This left fewer troops available to defend Malaya and Singapore, British colonies in Asia. A heavy price was paid for this when Japan entered the war.

Erwin Rommel

General Rommel became a legend in his own lifetime and achieved the distinction of being admired by the troops of opposing armies. Part of the reason for this was his style of directing operations from the front line and mixing informally with his soldiers. Generals were usually stationed well behind the front line and the ordinary soldier rarely glimpsed the men who were sending them into battle. Rommel wrote how 'when an attack is ordered the men must never be allowed to get the feeling that their casualties have been calculated in advance according to the laws of probability.'

General Rommel, second from the right, discussing battle plans with his staff in North Africa. Rommel's willingness to lead from the front line of battle, and his brilliant record as a tactician, won him the admiration of enemy soldiers as well as his own men.

War in the Balkans

Greece had been invaded by Italy in October 1940, and this triggered a series of reactions that further complicated the course of World War II. Why did Britain decide to divert troops from North Africa to Greece, and become involved in the region known as the Balkans? Churchill did not want Greece to be conquered, because if it were it would threaten British control of the eastern Mediterranean and Egypt. Germany was determined to prevent Britain from extending its influence in the Balkans, because from there it might provide support for southern Russia, which Hitler was about to invade.

Hitler decided to invade Greece and pressurized both Bulgaria and Hungary into accepting German troops in readiness for this invasion. Romania had already co-operated with Germany and, when Yugoslavia proved unwilling to do the same, Hitler ordered his forces to invade, in April 1941. The attack on Yugoslavia led to its break-up into separate states. Croatia became a fascist

Women, like these soldiers undergoing combat training for a partisan army in Yugoslavia, fought on the front line in eastern Europe. Neither Germany, Britain nor the USA used women as front-line fighters in World War II but in the USSR some drove tanks and died in combat.

state, where a quarter of a million people were murdered in three months. Muslims, Serbs and Christians became divided, some fighting the Germans while other groups fought each other. Internal conflicts also broke out in Bulgaria and Hungary.

After conquering Yugoslavia, Hitler went on successfully to invade Greece. Britain's air force in Greece was hopelessly outnumbered. It had fewer than 200 aircraft, most of which were out of date, against 1,000 belonging to Germany and Italy. The British tanks shipped to Greece were also fairly obsolete and many broke down on the rough terrain. The British were once more forced to evacuate, this time to the nearby island of Crete. This provided only a temporary refuge, for, in May 1941, German airborne troops parachuted from the skies over the island.

German soldiers in control of Crete after their successful but costly air-borne invasion of the island in May 1941. Nearly half of the nine thousand men dropped by parachute on the first day were killed.

Adolf Strauch was on holiday in Crete in the 1980s when the chance discovery of a helmet in the water brought back memories of past events there:

'The helmet in the sand reminds me of the 9,000 soldiers who, in May 1941, flew over the sea to capture the island. For the first time in the history of warfare the invaders came out of the sky. On the veranda of our bungalow I sat talking with my wife with the helmet, the product of my snorkelling, near me. My mind recalled things. Here in this peaceful area runs the old road to Rtheymnon. We fought in the nearby vineyards and olive groves and saw our first comrades die . . . They were late in jumping from the transport machines and fell in the sea. The weight of their equipment dragged them down. That was nearly 40 years ago and the helmet is lying here by my side.'

Source: James Lucas, *The Third Reich*

For the first time in history, victory was achieved by forces dropped by parachute, without support from troops on the ground. Arriving first in gliders, some 25,000 men dropped from the sky. They could be heard calling to each other as they floated down like 'beautiful little kicking dolls', in the words of someone who watched them.

Although their losses were high – more than 5,000 died – the German paratroops captured an airfield, which meant that aircraft could fly in reinforcements. Within six days, the Allies were defeated. Fewer than half the 40,000 Australian, British, Greek and New Zealand troops were evacuated; the rest were taken prisoner.

The Middle East

In the summer of 1941, the war spread even further and led to fighting in the Middle East. Like Egypt, Iraq was an independent country regarded by the British as a territory where they had a controlling interest. When a pro-German party seized power in Iraq, British troops overthrew the government and regained control.

The face of resignation and defeat belongs to a British soldier, now a prisoner of war, as he rests in the shadow of Mount Olympus in Greece in April 1941.

Before the war, the French had regarded Syria as territory under their control. After the fall of France it was under the control of the Vichy government, which collaborated with the Germans. The British, fighting in Iraq, were concerned that Syria might be of help to Germany in the Middle East. This was why Britain invaded Syria, with the assistance of a small French force that had refused to accept the Vichy government. After a short period of fighting, the Vichy French surrendered.

Hitler decided not to become involved in the Middle East. In June 1941, when around 2,000 men died in the fighting in Syria, Hitler's attention was elsewhere. He gave the order to launch another operation in the east of Europe, the invasion of the Soviet Union itself. This new campaign would change the whole course and the outcome of World War II – at a terrible price.

Marshal Petain, leader of the Vichy government of France, which collaborated with the Nazis. They failed to hold on to Syria when British troops invaded.

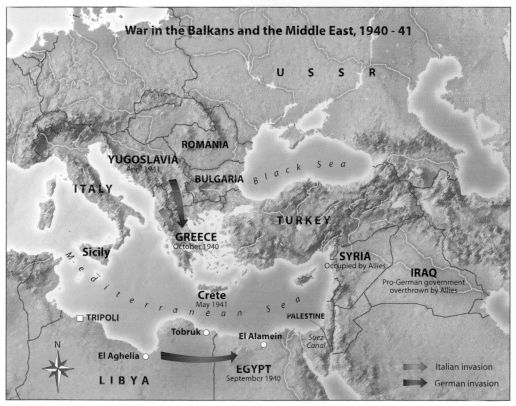

War in the Balkans and the Middle East, 1940 - 41

U S S R

ROMANIA

YUGOSLAVIA
April 1941

BULGARIA

Black Sea

ITALY

TURKEY

GREECE
October 1940

Sicily

SYRIA
Occupied by Allies

IRAQ
Pro-German government
overthrown by Allies

Mediterranean Sea

Crete
May 1941

PALESTINE

TRIPOLI

Tobruk

El Alamein

Suez
Canal

El Aghelia

EGYPT
September 1940

LIBYA

N

Italian invasion

German invasion

Barbarossa

The German invasion of the USSR began in the warmth of June 1941, but, by November, these soldiers were bogged down in the snow as they tried to fight their way towards Moscow.

A successful attack on the Soviet Union would bring that country's vast resources under Nazi control. Yet it was not the need for these resources that lay behind Hitler's determination to invade. Hitler and the Nazis were driven by a fierce hatred of communism, or Bolshevism as it was also called, and this is what the Soviet Union represented. The Soviet Union had been under communist power since 1917, when the ruling Tsar had been overthrown by those wishing to see wider distribution of property amongst citizens, with all people working for the good of the state. Hitler had signed the Nazi-Soviet Pact in 1939 only to provide security on his eastern borders while he was invading Poland and challenging Britain. As early as July 1940, his intention to invade the USSR was secretly announced to some of his top generals. The code name for the German attack was 'Barbarossa'.

Hitler knew the prize that awaited him if the USSR was conquered. He admired the British Empire and saw his own ambitions for Germany as imitating the achievements of the British: 'Let's learn from the English who, with 250,000 men in all, including 50,000 soldiers, govern 400 million Indians.' He went on to say that 'what India was for England, the territories of Russia will be for us.' Barbarossa was an attempt to extend power in Europe into world power.

A failure of imagination

For Hitler, the Nazi-Soviet Pact was a means of securing his eastern borders while he was occupied in the west. But what was in it for Stalin? The failure of Britain and France to take up his offer of a treaty against Germany in 1939 had left the Soviet leader vulnerable in Europe. The Nazi-Soviet Pact proved irresistible because it promised peace and security and the opportunity to divide up the spoils of eastern Europe with Germany. By early 1941, it was clear that Hitler was planning to invade the Soviet Union, but Stalin stubbornly refused to believe the obvious. His generals warned him but he was blind to the danger, convinced that Hitler would not risk a war in both eastern and western Europe. Stalin lacked the imagination to realize that, for Hitler, the prize was worth the risks of an invasion.

In December 1940, Hitler informed his war chiefs that the invasion of the Soviet Union would begin in the late spring of the following year. By June, Greece had been conquered and Rommel was in charge of the fighting in Africa. Everything was ready. The invasion of the USSR began on 22 June 1941.

Joseph Goebbels, the Nazi Minister for Propaganda, wrote in his diary on 16 June 1941:

'The Führer gives me a comprehensive explanation of the situation: the attack on Russia will begin as soon as all our troops are in position. This will be some time in the course of next week . . . The enemy will be driven back in one, smooth movement. The Führer estimates that the operation will take four months, I reckon on fewer. Bolshevism will collapse like a house of cards. We face victories unequalled in human history . . . The operation is also necessary from [Japan's] point of view. Tokyo would never become involved with the USA with Russia intact to her rear.'

Source: E. Taylor (ed.), *The Goebbels Diaries*

*The leader of the USSR, Joseph Stalin, resisted the wishes of his generals to mobilize troops for a possible German invasion.
'What do you want, a war?', he shouted in anger.*

The battle plan

Hitler and his generals were confident about defeating the USSR, even though they were invading an area twenty times larger than the land in western Europe they had conquered in 1940, with a front line that stretched for over 3,200 km. Their attack was divided into three main thrusts: in the north towards Leningrad; in the centre towards the capital, Moscow; and in the south into the Ukraine. The offensive involved a total of nearly 3.5 million men, 5,000 aircraft and 3,500 tanks. Fast-moving armoured formations, known as panzer divisions, roared into the Soviet Union. Whole divisions of the Red Army, taken by surprise and not yet equipped for a war on such a scale as this, were surrounded; German infantry followed up behind the panzers to complete the trap.

Hitler's prediction that the Russians 'will think a hurricane has hit them' proved correct at first. Nearly 300,000 men of the Red Army were captured around Minsk before the end of June and further successes followed. In the south more than half a million prisoners were taken near Kiev and the Crimea region was taken. In the north, Leningrad was besieged and the armies defending it seemed on the point of collapse. The Germans would eventually fail to capture either Leningrad or Moscow, but during the second half of 1941, their attack on the USSR seemed relentless.

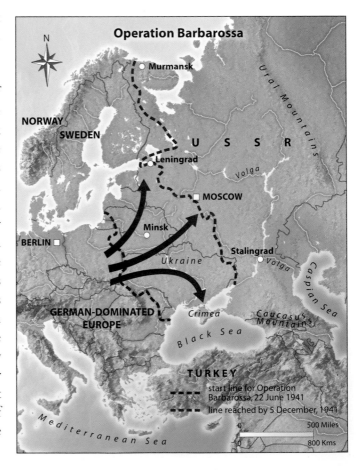

Operation Barbarossa

- - - - start line for Operation Barbarossa, 22 June 1941

- ■ - ■ line reached by 5 December, 1941

Just five of the many millions of citizens of the USSR who died during the war. For every member of the armed forces killed during World War II, two civilians died.

Barbarism

The SS had special killing squads, the *Einsatzgruppen*, which had already been in operation in Poland and were now let loose in the Soviet Union. Hundreds of thousands of Jews and Russians were murdered, yet the killing squads only numbered about 3,000 and could not have killed so many without the support of the regular German army. Army chiefs knew that Communist Party officials in the Red Army and Jews were to be executed and they helped the *Einsatzgruppen* by rounding up victims. They also ordered their troops to co-operate with the SS in shooting all partisans. Public hangings took place, with the bodies left to rot, and it was not unheard of for wounded Russians to be buried alive.

Heinrich Himmler, the head of the SS, which was responsible for crushing the enemies of Nazism, made this comment in April 1943:

'We have only one task, to stand and pitilessly to lead this race-battle . . .The reputation for horror and terror which preceded us we want never to allow to diminish. The world may call us what it will.'

Source: Richard Overy, *Russia's War*

Just as shocking were the conditions in which Soviet prisoners were left to die. They were often simply herded behind barbed wire out in the open and hemmed in by guard dogs that received larger rations than the prisoners themselves. Soviet prisoners suffered a higher death rate than any other group of prisoners in World War II.

The siege of Leningrad

In the besieged city of Leningrad, living conditions were terrible. Food rations dropped to 250 g of bread a day for workers and soldiers; half that for everyone else. A doctor visited a home in January 1942:

'My eyes beheld a horrible sight. A dark room covered with frost, puddles of water on the floor. Lying across some chairs was the corpse of a fourteen-year-old boy. In a baby carriage was a second corpse, that of a tiny infant. On the bed lay the owner of the room — dead. At her side, rubbing her chest with a towel, stood her eldest daughter . . . In one day she lost her mother, a son and a brother who perished from hunger and cold.'

Source: Richard Overy, *Russia's War*

Fury at the barbarism unleashed on them by Germany produced a tremendous spirit of resistance among Soviet citizens and soldiers — it was probably a stronger motivating force than loyalty to Stalin, their leader. The Soviet armies did not totally collapse and partisans organized additional resistance. Factories that were vital to the war effort were dismantled and moved thousands of kilometres east, beyond the Ural Mountains, where they were out of reach of the invading German armies. Two such factories were reassembled and combined with a tractor factory to form a new, colossal tank factory named Tankograd. This was where the famous, diesel-powered T-34 tank was built.

The T-34

Distinguished by sturdy, sloping armour that was difficult for shells to penetrate, and running at 40 kph for about 450 km before it needed refuelling, the T-34 so impressed German generals that they wanted to copy it for their own armies. German engineers refused because they could not believe that 'backward' Russians could develop a tank technology superior to their own.

The Russian T-34 tank, shown here advancing to the front line through Leningrad, surprised the Germans by its strength and fire power. Over 40,000 were produced, one of the most important weapons in World War II.

Left *Women in the besieged Russian city of Leningrad (now St Petersburg) dismantle the wood from a bomb-damaged house.*

45

As the German forces stretched out to cover the three thrusts of the attack – towards Leningrad, Moscow and the Ukraine – the relentless pace of the onslaught slowed. Hitler insisted on splitting the central force to support the attack in the south, so the advance on Moscow was delayed. Tanks then had to be diverted from the attack on Leningrad to support the central thrust towards Moscow, and Leningrad was saved.

When the move forward to capture Moscow finally started in October, it was too late. Heavy rain and constant churning by military vehicles turned the badly made roads to mud, slowing the German advance. In Moscow, a brilliant general named Zhukov took over the defence of the capital. Experienced troops, as well as tanks and aircraft, were recalled from the Soviet Union's eastern borders to help protect the city.

Georgi Konstantinovich Zhukov

Zhukov was born in 1897 into a shoemaker's family in a village close to Moscow and before he was 20 he was conscripted into the cavalry. After his country's revolution in 1918 he remained in the army and became a patriotic communist. In January 1941, he suddenly found himself promoted to Chief of the General Staff. There was no higher military rank and, once the Germans invaded, Zhukov knew that failure to halt their advance would cost him his life. He was a ruthless but brilliant commander who, more than anyone else, was responsible for saving both Leningrad (now St Petersburg) and Moscow from the Nazis.

Marshal Zhukov masterminded the defence of Moscow and Leningrad against the Germans. One of the most brilliant generals of the war, he would later lead the Soviet army to Berlin.

By November the German advance had been halted. Troops were forced to spend the winter in the open without proper clothing, as temperatures plummeted below -40°C. The German armies encamped around Moscow could see the spires of the Kremlin through binoculars but this was the closest they would ever get to it. The Soviet Union had not been defeated. Hitler's plan had failed. And, in December 1941, the USA entered the war.

Hitler's confidence in being able to defeat the USSR before the winter of 1941 meant that he failed to plan for winter clothing and winter supplies. This German propaganda photograph taken in Russia does not convey the horror of what awaited soldiers.

Numbers too large

The numbers of soldiers and civilians who died in the attack on the USSR are so large that it becomes difficult to imagine the scale of human suffering involved.

- Two-thirds of the 20 million deaths among fighting forces in World War II occurred during the invasion of the USSR.

- More than 2 million German soldiers died invading the USSR.

- An estimated 13 million died defending the USSR. One million people, one in three of the city's population, died during the siege of Leningrad.

- 60 per cent of the 3 million Russians taken prisoner in 1941 were dead by early 1942.

- Half a million Jews were murdered within the first six months of the invasion.

- 58 per cent of Soviet prisoners died; the equivalent rate for German prisoners was 30 per cent.

Japan attacks

A war for the world

The war that started in 1939 was caused by Germany's attempt to expand outside its national borders and dominate Europe. Although the entry of Italy into the war spread the area of fighting to Africa and the Middle East, the war remained a conflict between European powers. Two developments turned it into a world war and a battle for world leadership. The first was Barbarossa, Hitler's invasion of the USSR – a German empire that stretched from western Europe to the far reaches of eastern Russia could challenge the USA and Japan, if necessary. The second was the involvement of Japan and the USA.

Franklin Roosevelt led the USA into World War II but died three weeks before the surrender of Germany.

Although the USA was actively opposed to Hitler, President Roosevelt and his government had to deal with the legacy of isolationism and the fact that public opinion was very much opposed to joining the war. This meant that, in 1939, the USA was not ready to conduct a major war, either in military or political terms. The lack of military readiness could be solved by getting rearmament quickly under way but the political situation presented more of a problem. Opinion polls showed that 80 per cent of the population wanted to stay out of the war and this acted as a brake on Roosevelt's ability to intervene directly.

Long before it became involved in fighting, however, the USA was already playing an important role in World War II, through its support of Britain. Although Britain seemed very powerful, with an empire and a willingness to challenge Hitler, the country was really in serious decline as a world power. By early 1941, Britain was virtually bankrupt and unable to pay for the vital supplies of oil and other materials from the USA that were needed to continue the war. The Lend-Lease Act, by which the USA loaned or leased equipment to Britain with a promise of payment after the war, was a commitment by the USA to prevent the takeover of Europe by Hitler's Germany.

The US government also faced a problem in Asia where Japan was making it increasingly clear that American attempts to limit its power would be resisted. Like Germany, Japan also sought expansion, into China and the territories in the Far East that were colonies of European empires. The USA was keen to maintain and strengthen its own influence in the Pacific region, especially in China. In the course of 1941, attempts at a diplomatic solution to this conflict of interests failed. War became increasingly likely.

When all these powerful countries – Germany, the USSR, Japan and the USA – were at war, the stakes were very high. The victors would be in a position to dominate the world. Their power would be unchallengeable.

Japan sent troops into Shanghai, in China, in 1937, in an effort to bring China into the Japanese Empire.

49

Japanese expansion

In Japan in the late 1930s, military and business groups were calling for national expansion. Since 1931, Japan had controlled Manchuria and, in 1937, an incident when Chinese troops fired on Japanese forces near

US leaders saw China as a desirable ally in the struggle against Japan, as shown in this propaganda poster of 1942.

Beijing led to an invasion of mainland China. The Japanese government also made it clear that the Washington Treaty of 1922, which limited the size of the Japanese fleet, was no longer going to be accepted. This was a direct challenge to US interests in the Pacific region.

The USA retaliated by providing massive loans to China, to help finance a war of resistance against the Japanese. In the same way that the USA opposed Hitler by providing aid to Britain, there was now also a willingness to support China as a means of containing Japan.

The US Pacific Fleet was moved from the west coast of the US mainland to Pearl Harbor in Hawaii, so that it could take action more quickly in the western Pacific if this became necessary. In July 1940, the USA also placed an embargo on the sale of aviation fuel to Japan, as well as on some types of scrap iron and steel.

Hitler's successes in Europe in 1940 increased Japanese belligerence because, with France defeated and Britain apparently on the verge of collapse, the South-east Asian possessions of these European powers became very vulnerable. Cambodia and Vietnam, known then as French Indo-China, were taken over by Japan in September 1940, and Thailand was forced to accept Japanese military bases. At the same time, the Three-Power Act was signed between Japan, Germany and Italy, making it clear that, if Britain were defeated, her possessions in South-east Asia would also fall to Japan.

A US Marine described the attitude of many people towards the growing danger in the Pacific region:

'Virtually all Americans were descended from European immigrants. They had studied Continental geography in school. When commentators told them that Nazi spearheads were knifing here and there, they needed no maps; they all had maps in their minds. Oriental geography, on the other hand, was (and still is) a mystery to most of them. Yet the Japanese had been fighting in China since 1931 . . . Europe, we thought, was where the danger lay. Indeed, one of my reasons for joining the Marine Corps was that, in 1918, the Marines had been among the first US troops to fight the Germans. Certainly I never dreamt I would wind up on the other side of the world.'

Source: William Manchester, *Goodbye, Darkness*

However, the most tempting possession in the region was central Indonesia, which was rich in the natural resources the Japanese needed. Central Indonesia was then known as the Dutch East Indies and it was part of the empire of the Netherlands. The Netherlands had been conquered by Hitler in 1940 but the Dutch government had fled and based themselves in London. The Japanese demanded large supplies of much-needed oil, as well as rubber and tin, from the Dutch East Indies, but the Dutch government refused. By July 1941, the Japanese had decided to take the Dutch East Indies by force. They were fully aware that by doing so they risked open war with the USA.

'Indonesia must be free! Work and fight for it!' states this Dutch poster objecting to Japanese expansion in the Dutch East Indies.

The spy who loved Russia

The USSR and Japan were not on friendly terms and, in 1938 and 1939, had clashed in the east, where the USSR shared a border with Japanese-occupied Manchuria. The possibility of war kept Soviet troops in the region on full alert.

Richard Sorge, a Soviet spy working in Tokyo, was able to gather secret information about Japanese government decisions. In 1941, he informed Moscow that Japan was going to attack southwards and that the Soviet Union's eastern border was safe. This allowed armaments and 200,000 troops to be recalled to Moscow, where they played a vital role in pushing back the German army from the suburbs of the Soviet capital. Moscow's survival, which was crucial to the eventual defeat of Germany, might not have happened without the information provided by Sorge. Richard Sorge was arrested soon after passing on this information. The Japanese executed him in 1944.

General Hideki Tojo served in Manchuria, became Minister of War in 1940 and, from 1941, was Japan's prime minister. After the war, he was tried as a war criminal and was sentenced to death in 1948.

Countdown to war

During the second half of 1941, a deadly game of diplomacy was played out between the USA and Japan. When the USA learnt of the plan to seize the Dutch East Indies, oil sales to Japan were stopped and Japanese assets in the USA frozen. The British and Dutch took similar action. This raised the stakes to a dangerous level because the survival of the Japanese economy was now threatened.

In September, Japan's leaders approved military plans for simultaneous attacks on Pearl Harbor and Southeast Asia, and the following month saw the resignation of Japanese politicians who wished to avoid war. General Tojo, who had been Minister of War, now assumed overall control of the Japanese government on behalf of the military.

Relations between the USA and Japan had now reached crisis point and only last-minute diplomacy could avoid all-out war. Negotiations between the two countries did take place in November, with each side hoping that the other side would make a concession. However, Britain and China were not keen to support a compromise deal and, when the USA insisted on a full Japanese withdrawal from China, the chances of a negotiated settlement evaporated. On 1 December, the decision to go to war was finally taken at the Imperial Palace in Tokyo.

'Climb Mount Niitaka 1208'

'Climb Mount Niitaka 1208' was the coded message transmitted to the Japanese fleet in the Pacific on the day after the 1 December meeting in Tokyo. Niitaka is the highest mountain in Japan and 1208 referred to 8 December. The message meant that on that date the Japanese forces were to carry out a pre-emptive strike against the US Pacific Fleet at Pearl Harbor. (The date in Hawaii was 7 December, as the islands lie on the other side of the international date line from Japan.) This was designed to put the US fleet out of action so that further Japanese attacks in South-east Asia could take place unopposed. A fleet of six aircraft-carriers, with 14 other ships and eight oil tankers to allow refuelling, had set off secretly from Japan into the north Pacific. On

the carriers were torpedo bombers that were to launch their torpedoes against US ships in the harbour and then ditch in the sea and await rescue. The ships also carried Zeros and other aircraft that would bomb and machine-gun the base before returning to the aircraft-carriers.

The Japanese fleet did not expect to reach its target position, over 320 km north of Hawaii, without being spotted at some stage, but the Americans did not have an aerial reconnaissance system operating from Hawaii. The Japanese ships were never spotted. Their aircraft took off unopposed and tuned in their direction-finders on the commercial radio station that was broadcasting to American servicemen in Hawaii.

Pearl Harbor, Hawaii, in 1941, shortly before the Japanese attack on 7 December. This view would have greeted the Japanese pilots on that Sunday morning.

The Japanese Zero

One of the most effective planes of World War II was the Mitsubishi A6M, more commonly known by both the Japanese and the Allies as the Zero. It was a single-seat plane and the version that was flown from aircraft carriers had folding wingtips for ease of storage. It could even be unbolted and stored in two halves if necessary. The Zero achieved fame due to its light weight, which helped to give it a range of 1,600 km, and its unusual manoeuvrability, which was superior to that of any other plane at the time. First used in China in 1940, more than 10,000 Zeros were produced.

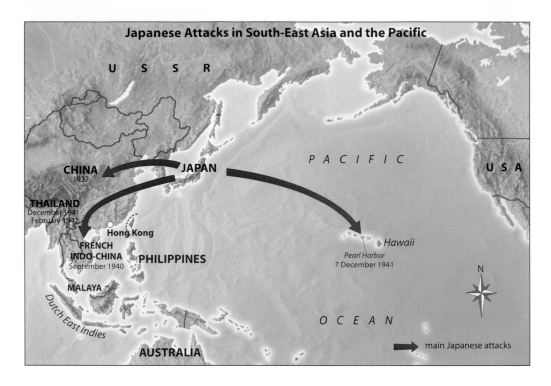

On the morning of 7 December, military leaders in Washington, USA, had just received the last part of an official communication from Japan, which concluded that 'it is impossible to reach an agreement through further negotiations'. Japanese warships had been seen gathering near Malaya and the Dutch East Indies and it seemed certain that these territories would be attacked. However, the Japanese plan to launch an airborne attack from ships against Pearl Harbor itself was so original and daring that it was never considered as a possibility.

Attack on Pearl Harbor

At 7.30 a.m., Hawaii time, a motorcycle despatch rider on the island of Honolulu set off to deliver the warning from Washington to the military chiefs at Pearl Harbor. He was still on his motorbike when Japanese planes launched their attack at 7.55 a.m., bombing the airfields to disable American aircraft. It has gone down in history that the attack was launched with the cry of 'Tora! Tora! Tora!' ('Tora' is Japanese for 'tiger') but in fact the term arose accidentally from the Morse code that was used to signal that surprise had been achieved.

More than 180 planes came over Pearl Harbor in the first of two attacking waves, and only caution by Japanese commanders prevented a third attack that could have inflicted more serious damage. Two American fighter planes did manage to take off and bring down six Japanese aircraft. It was later suggested that one of the pilots should be awarded the Medal of Honor, but the idea was turned down because he had taken off without orders.

The two-hour attack appeared to have been an unqualified success. The Japanese lost only 10 per cent of their aircraft but sank or crippled 21 US ships, with the loss of more than 2,500 US lives. However, the four aircraft-carriers of the Pacific Fleet were not in the harbour at the time and therefore survived; 18 of the 21 bomb-damaged ships were eventually repaired; and over 4 million tonnes of fuel held in storage escaped being ignited by the attack.

The Arizona *Sinks*

The Japanese used heavy bombs against the strong steel battleships they were attacking and one of these 795 kg bombs hit the deck of the *Arizona* and ignited more than 500,000 kg of explosives. A seaman on board recalled what happened:

'We took a hit on the starboard side, and it went right into the magazines and aviation gasoline. There was a terrific explosion, and a fireball went into the air 400 feet [122m] or more. Of the 50 or 60 men manning the station where I was, I think only about six of us survived. I was burned over 60 per cent of my body. The Vestal, a repair ship that was tied up alongside us, threw us a line and we went across hand over hand, 45 feet [13.5 m] in the air.'

Source: *Life* magazine, Special Pearl Harbor issue, Fall 1991

After the Japanese attack, newsreels and photographs like this one of a burning battleship in Pearl Harbor transformed American public opinion. Isolationism became a spent force and the country united behind Roosevelt's commitment to the war.

Japanese victories

The attack on Pearl Harbor over, the main task of replacing the European empires in Asia with a Japanese empire got under way. Battle-hardened from the war in China, experienced Japanese troops landed in the north of Malaya and across the border in Thailand. In a blistering campaign lasting ten weeks, they completely outwitted and outfought the Indian, British and Australian forces, which withdrew to the island of Singapore at the southern tip of the Malayan peninsula.

British military leaders were handicapped in various ways, not least by a sense of being racially superior to the Japanese, which gave them a false sense of security. The sinking of the only two British battleships in the region by bombers and torpedo bombers, together with an inadequate supply of aircraft, gave the Japanese mastery of the sea and air. In February 1942, the British surrendered Singapore and their force of 100,000 soldiers to a Japanese force of 30,000 who were down to their last supplies of ammunition.

British soldiers surrender in Singapore. Captured soldiers were marched to a prison camp and forced to make a promise not to try to escape.

The Japanese victory was a humiliating defeat for the British in more ways than one. From the island of Penang, in the north of Malaya, the secret evacuation of 'European women and children only' took place overnight without other citizens being informed. In Singapore, some inexperienced troops lost their discipline and there were scenes of looting and attempts to flee on ships trying to take civilians to safety.

The USS Shaw, receiving a direct hit on her ammunition store, explodes at Pearl Harbor. This was the dramatic scene marking the USA's entry into World War II.

The world at war

Britain's defeat, along with the successful attack on Pearl Harbor, put Japan in a commanding position in the western Pacific and Asia. Their desperate need for fuel was solved by the conquest of the oil-rich Dutch East Indies, while Malaya provided plentiful supplies of natural rubber and tin. Within a week of Pearl Harbor, Germany and Italy had declared war on the USA. The world was now truly at war.

Date list

1918	World War I ends.
1919	Treaty of Versailles signed.
1922	Mussolini comes to power in Italy. Washington Treaty signed.
1929–33	Great Depression
1931	Japan invades Manchuria in China.
1933	Hitler becomes Chancellor of Germany.
1935	Italy invades Abyssinia in Africa.
1936	German troops occupy the Rhineland.
1937	Japanese troops invade China.
1938 **March**	*Anschluss* takes place, uniting Germany and Austria.
September	Hitler takes over the Sudetenland area of Czechoslovakia.
1939 **March**	Hitler occupies Bohemia-Moravia in Czechoslovakia.
August	Nazi–Soviet Pact is signed.
1 September	Germany invades Poland.
3 September	Britain and France declare war on Germany.

1940 **April-June**	Germany conquers Denmark, Norway, the Netherlands, Belgium and France.
26 May– 4 June	British troops evacuated from Dunkirk in France.
10 June	Italy declares war on Britain and France.
July–Sept	Battle of Britain takes place.
September	Bombing campaign against British cities (the 'Blitz') begins. Germany, Italy and Japan sign Three-Power (Tripartite) Pact. Italy invades Egypt. Japan occupies French Indo-China.
28 October	Italy invades Greece.
1941 **February**	Allied successes against Italian forces in North Africa.
April	Lend-Lease Act between Britain and USA signed
6 April	Germany invades Yugoslavia.
May	Allied forces in Crete defeated.
22 June	Operation Barbarossa – the German invasion of the USSR launched.
November	German advance on Moscow halted.
7 December	Japanese attack Pearl Harbor.
11 December	Germany and Italy declare war on USA.

Glossary

Anschluss a German term, meaning 'joining together', that refers to Austria's voluntary submission to German rule in March 1938.

appeasement the policy towards Germany that was followed by Britain and France in the 1930s; it involved giving in to Hitler's demands for the restoration of territory lost under the Treaty of Versailles.

Balkans the region of south-east Europe that includes Greece, Bosnia, Croatia and Serbia.

Barbarossa the German code name for the planned attack on the USSR.

Blitz taken from the German word *Blitzkrieg* ('lightning war'), the Blitz became the term for Germany's sustained campaign of bombing British cities that started in September 1940.

convoy a group of merchant ships (or other vehicles) travelling together

demilitarized a term used to describe an area in which it is forbidden to station troops.

diplomacy negotiations between one state and another, designed to maintain friendly relations and resolve any disputes peacefully.

embargo a ban, for example on the sale of certain goods to a specific country.

Fascism a form of government favouring obedience to authority, that crushes political opposition with the force of state power, such as Hitler's Germany or Mussolini's Italy.

Führer German for 'leader' and part of the title adopted by Hitler in 1934.

genocide The deliberate extermination of a people or nation.

infantry soldiers who fight on foot using rifles and other small arms.

isolationism a policy of withdrawing from international politics, as practised by the USA towards Europe after World War I.

Luftwaffe the German air force.

pact an agreement or a treaty, like the Nazi–Soviet Pact of 1939.

panzer a German armoured vehicle, especially a tank.

partisans fighters who carry out attacks such as small-scale raids, or sabotage attacks on enemy forces, but who do not belong to a regular army.

pincer movement an encircling movement by two wings of a force, converging on the enemy.

pre-emptive intended to disable an enemy by striking before the enemy can attack.

propaganda organized publicity to promote a particular view.

Resources

protectionist the term used for a policy of imposing high taxes (duties) on imported goods, thus making them more expensive in comparison with goods produced by a country's own industries.

radar a method of identifying the position of distant objects using radio waves.

ratify confirm or accept an agreement or treaty formally.

reparations compensation payments.

Russia the leading power and the largest union republic in the Union of Soviet Socialist Republics (USSR).

Slavs peoples of central and eastern Europe who speak Slavonic languages such as Russian and Polish.

SS the *Schutzstaffeln,* a special organization devoted to the application of Nazi ideas such as the extermination of the Jews.

Suez Canal a vital sea-route through Egypt linking the Mediterranean with the Red Sea, which allows ships to travel to the Far East without having to go right round Africa.

U-boat German submarine.

USSR the Union of Soviet Socialist Republics (also known as the Soviet Union), a country formed from the territories of the Russian Empire after the Bolshevik revolution of 1917, which lasted until the late 1980s.

Sources

Total War (Volume 1) by Peter Calvocoressi (Penguin, 1989)

Blood, Tears and Folly by Len Deighton (Pimlico, 1995)

The Origins of the Second World War in Asia and the Pacific by Akira Iriye (Longman, 1987)

A World in Flames by Martin Kitchen (Longman, 1990)

The Meaning of the Second World War by Ernest Mandel (Verso, 1986)

The Origins of the Second World War by R J Overy (Longman, 1987)

The Second World War by A J P Taylor (Penguin, 1975)

Acknowledgements

The publishers wish to thank the following for permission to quote extracts in this book: Chatto & Windus for *What Did You Do In The War, Mummy?* by Mavis Nicholson; Pearson Education Limited for *The Origins of the Second World War* by R J Overy; J M Dent for *Dunkirk, The Great Escape* by A J Barker; Arms & Armour, Cassell & Co for *Experiences of War: The Third Reich* by James Lucas; Penguin/Viking for *Private Words* by Ronald Blythe; Penguin/Hamish Hamilton for *The Goebbels Diaries*, 1939-41 ed. E Taylor; Penguin/Michael Joseph for *Goodbye Darkness* by William Manchester; Penguin for *Russia's War* by Richard Overy.

Books to read:

The Second World War by A J P Taylor (Penguin). A very readable account of the war, generously illustrated with colour photographs, which combines facts with opinions.

Blood, Tears and Folly by Len Deighton (Pimlico). The novelist Len Deighton has written a number of engaging books - fiction and non-fiction - about World War II and this is one of the best accounts of the first two years of the war. Also worth looking at are his *Fighter: The True Story of the Battle of Britain* and *Blitzkrieg: From the Rise of Hitler to the Fall of Dunkirk*.

I Have Lived a Thousand Years by Livia Bitton-Jackson (Aladdin). An emotional but truthful account of a young Hungarian girl who finds her life shattered by the invasion of her country by Hitler's Germany.

World War II: Facts, Things to Make, Activities by Rachel Wright (Franklin Watts). This book is full of practical ideas for craft work related to the war.

The Origins of the Second World War by Peter Allen (Wayland). This history book, aimed at young teenagers, covers the background and course of events that led to the outbreak of the war.

A People's War by Peter Lewis (Thames Methuen). A close look at the civilian's experience of the war. The first few chapters cover many of the events that are looked at in this book.

Internet Resources:

The Imperial War Museum in London has a web site at www.iwm.org.uk/ which is well worth looking at for general information about the war and areas of special interest to the museum.

Using the search facility on your web browser, enter World War II in the subject box and look at some of the web sites that are listed. One site that is worth looking at, and which contains links to other relevant sites, is: http://webpub.alleg.edu/student/p/paynes/war.html

Other resources and activities:

The Times Atlas of the Second World War is a huge book that is worth dipping into for its highly detailed maps of the various campaigns and battles of World War II.

The Imperial War Museum has a mail order service for literature on World War II, including facsimile packs, study document packs, archive film videos, audio tapes and posters.
The Imperial War Museum, Lambeth Road, London, SE1 6HZ

Videos

Blitzkrieg: Lightning War; Battle of Britain and *Target Pearl Harbor* are three videos covering some of the major events of the early part of the war and containing mostly original film of that time.
DD Video, 5 Churchill Court, 58 Station Road, North Harrow, Middlesex, HA2 7SA.

Index